POMPEII

Richard Platt

Illustrated by Manuela Cappon

KINGFISHER

Pompeii

Between the dark shadow of a mountain and the sparkling waters of the Bay of Naples there once lay a lively, bustling town. Pompeii was much like other towns on Italy's western shore. Greeks had settled here, and they were joined by other foreign settlers in the third century BCE. In later years, its citizens included soldiers of the Roman empire that ruled the Mediterranean lands of southern Europe.

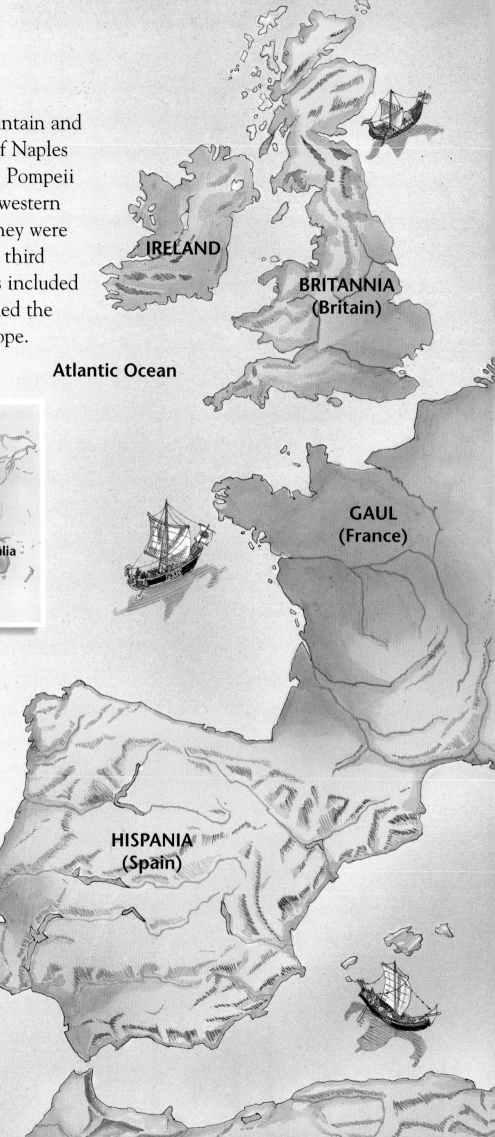

IRELAND

BRITANNIA
(Britain)

Atlantic Ocean

North
America

Asia

Europe

Africa

South
America

Australia

GAUL
(France)

Pompeii is on the 'shin' of boot-shaped Italy, in the middle of the Mediterranean Sea. Two thousand years ago, Pompeii was thriving. Its wealthiest citizens owned beautiful homes, luxuriously decorated. Slaves and poorer people worked in its houses, shops, docks and workshops.

But in 79CE disaster struck. The volcanic mountain, Vesuvius, exploded. Life in Pompeii suddenly ended. Dust and ash fell from the sky, preserving everything it covered. This turned Pompeii into a perfect, tragic snapshot of Roman life.

HISPANIA
(Spain)

GERMANIA
(Germany)

Pompeii in the 1st century CE

Mount Vesuvius

ILYRICUM

DACIA

ITALY

•Pompeii

Bay of Naples

MACEDONIA

Mediterranean Sea

Pompeii timeline

around 900 BCE Vesuvius erupts, covering the area in ash

6th century BCE Oscan (northern Italian) people settle and build Pompeii's first walls

5th century BCE Pompeii's people build new, higher walls to protect their farms

4th century BCE Rome conquers the Bay of Naples

around 320BCE Vesuvius erupts. It then goes quiet for almost 400 years

3rd century BCE Many more Greeks settle in Pompeii

2nd century BCE Pompeii is an important port, trading with Greece and elsewhere

146BCE Rome defeats its great rival Carthage in the last of three Punic wars

1st century BCE Forest covers sleeping Vesuvius, including its cratered top

89BCE A Roman army crushes a rebellion in Pompeii

81BCE Retired soldiers settle in Pompeii, making it a Roman city

44BCE Julius Caesar, dictator of Rome, is murdered

59CE After a riot at a gladiator contest, the amphitheatre in Pompeii is shut

62CE An earthquake destroys many of Pompeii's buildings

64CE Another, less damaging tremor rocks the region

79CE, August 24th Thousands die when Vesuvius erupts, burying Pompeii in ash

80CE Roman emperor Titus visits Pompeii after the eruption

80CE onwards Pompeii's surviving people dig to salvage what they can of their homes

1000CE Pompeii has been forgotten; people now call the place 'la Città'

1600CE Digging of a new canal reveals traces of Pompeii

1631CE Vesuvius erupts with as much violence as in 79CE

1689CE Workers digging a new well discover remains of Pompeii

1748CE Excavators begin digging for Pompeii's treasures

1763CE A stone carved with 'Pompeii' is dug up, identifying the town

1775CE More careful excavations replace treasure hunts at Pompeii

1860CE Archaeologist Giuseppe Fiorelli begins scientific study of Pompeii

2000CE Work begins to dig up the one-third of Pompeii that is still buried

What do these dates mean?
'CE' means Common Era. This is the period of measured time that begins with 1CE (or AD1).

'BCE' means Before Common Era, and refers to any dates before 1CE. For example, 100BCE means '100 years before the Common Era'.

900BCE

500BCE

400BCE

300BCE

200BCE

100BCE

1CE

1000CE

2000CE

Contents

The pages that follow trace the history of a typical house in Pompeii. You can see how the house grew as the city flourished. You can watch it crumble in flames and ash with the rest of the city when Vesuvius erupted. And you can discover how it was found again and restored, many centuries later.

The city under attack
page 16

Farms and crafts
page 8

The house prospers
page 12

A growing city
page 20

380BCE **150**BCE **89**BCE **10**CE

750BCE **300**BCE **100**BCE **82**BCE

A humble hut
page 6

Inside the atrium
page 14

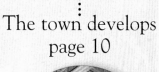

The town develops
page 10

After the war
page 18

What does this symbol mean?
This vase shows you where the house is in each busy city scene, so that you can follow its story through time.

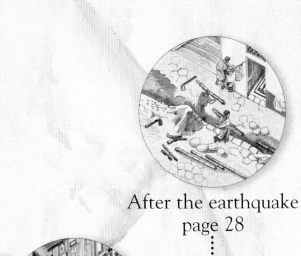

After the earthquake
page 28

Treasure hunters
page 36

The house at
its peak
page 22

The eruption
page 30

Romantic ruin
page 40

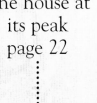

60CE **70**CE **79**CE **1750**CE *Today*

60CE **62**CE

A banquet
page 24

100CE

A city buried
page 32

1689CE **1870**CE

Studying the ruins
page 38

The earthquake
page 26

Pompeii
forgotten
page 34

A humble hut
750BCE

Pompeii begins as little more than a group of farms. Rough walls enclose the oldest of them. Already the town is too big for its boundaries, and some families have started to farm land nearby. Here, beyond the walls, one house stands out. Though just a hut, it is at the centre of the most prosperous farm.

The land around the farm supplied almost everything needed to build the hut. Solid tree trunks form the frame. Ropes that tie the roof timbers together are made of twisted plant fibres. Stalks from the emmer crop and reeds cut from nearby riverbanks provide the thatched roof. Only the thatcher's metal tools were not made on the farm.

woodland provides timber and foraging areas for pigs

fishing boats moor at the nearby harbour

Grapes are harvested from the vines grown at the foot of Mount Vesuvius, and are used for making wine.

a hole at the top of each hut lets out smoke from a cooking fire inside

a boy chases birds away from the emmer crop

the emmer grain is used to make wheat for flour

reapers cut only the heads of stalks to harvest the grain, so the left-over straw can be used for thatching

emmer straw is cut and used for thatching

a shovel made entirely of wood

metal tools are the most valuable of the farmers' possessions

thorn bushes provide natural barbed wire

the fence keeps pigs in and wolves out

the volcano has been quiet for many years

Farmers make offerings to their gods at the temples of the old town, in the southwestern area of Pompeii.

forests cover the lower slopes of Mount Vesuvius

vines are grown at the foot of the slopes

grapevines

this small hut is the beginning of a house that will stand on this site for more than 800 years

the roads in this part of Pompeii are simple tracks

sheep provide milk as well as meat and wool

vegetable plot for growing cabbages, leeks, turnips and onions

a new thatch is being added to this hut

tame pigs run to the sound of the herder's horn

The farming family works hard, for they must do everything by hand. Even the youngest child helps, scaring away birds and picking bugs off the food plants. If there is enough rain, they will eat well again this year – as long as they can keep the wolves away from the pigs, and wild boar out of the grain!

7

Farms and crafts 380BCE

As Pompeii grows and its people thrive, it begins to look less like farmland. Roads and tracks have created a grid of roughly equal-sized plots. In this northern area of Pompeii, farmers still grow crops and raise animals within the town walls. But as well as farming, the town is now home to a new kind of work.

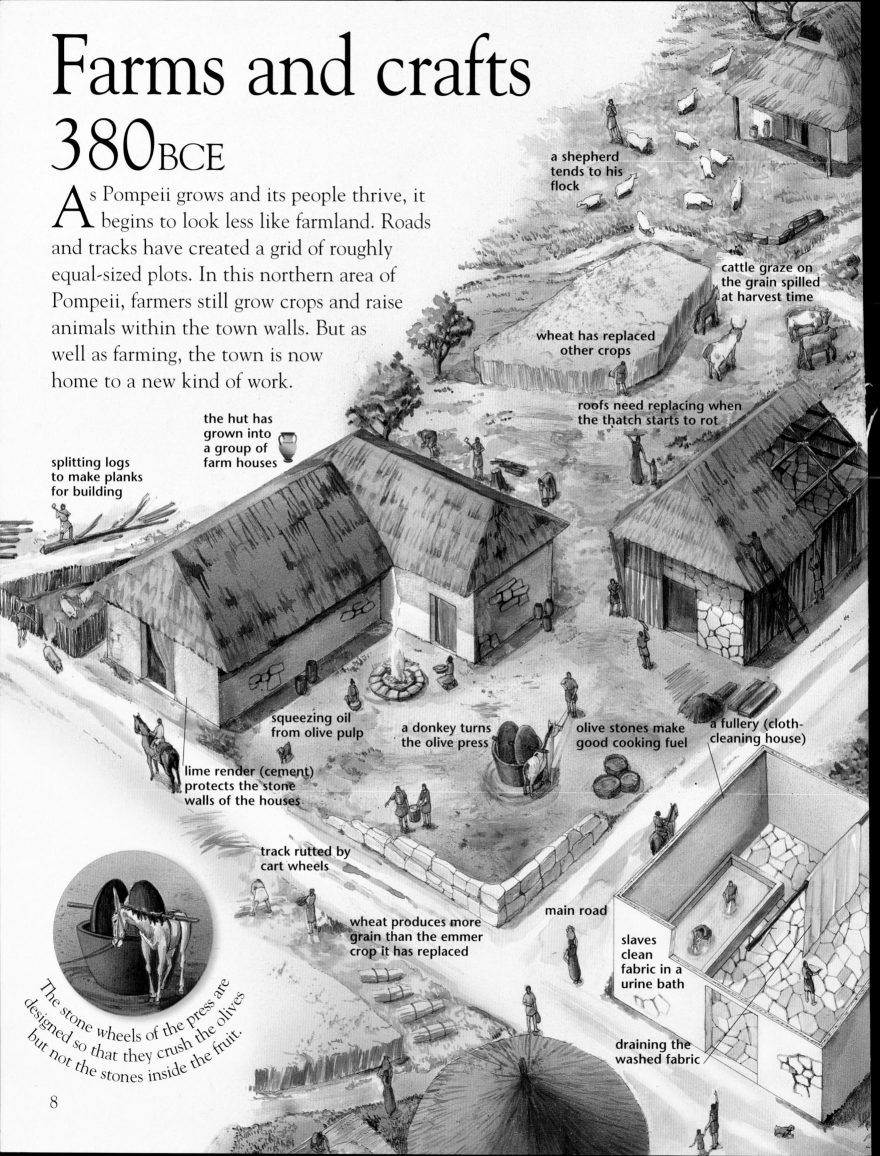

a shepherd tends to his flock

cattle graze on the grain spilled at harvest time

wheat has replaced other crops

roofs need replacing when the thatch starts to rot

the hut has grown into a group of farm houses

splitting logs to make planks for building

squeezing oil from olive pulp

a donkey turns the olive press

olive stones make good cooking fuel

a fullery (cloth-cleaning house)

lime render (cement) protects the stone walls of the houses

track rutted by cart wheels

main road

wheat produces more grain than the emmer crop it has replaced

slaves clean fabric in a urine bath

draining the washed fabric

The stone wheels of the press are designed so that they crush the olives but not the stones inside the fruit.

8

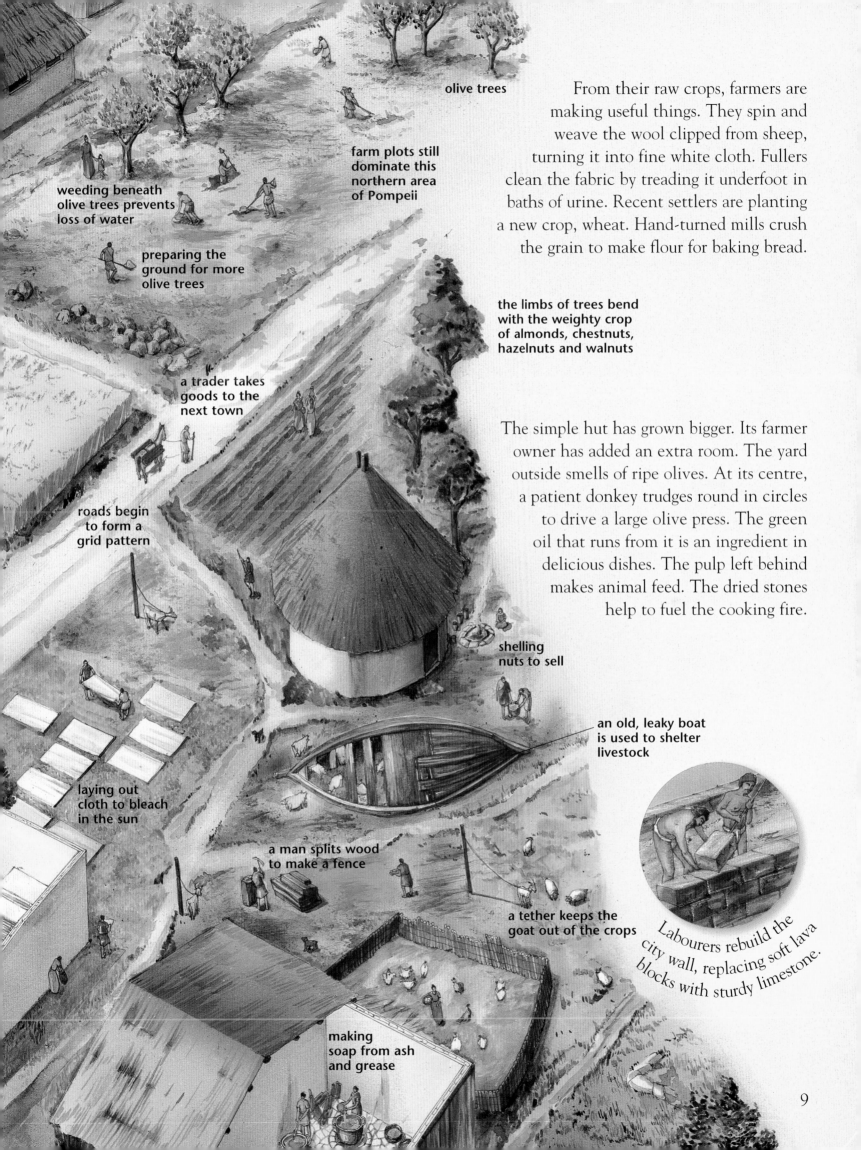

olive trees

weeding beneath
olive trees prevents
loss of water

farm plots still
dominate this
northern area
of Pompeii

preparing the
ground for more
olive trees

a trader takes
goods to the
next town

roads begin
to form a
grid pattern

laying out
cloth to bleach
in the sun

a man splits wood
to make a fence

the limbs of trees bend
with the weighty crop
of almonds, chestnuts,
hazelnuts and walnuts

shelling
nuts to sell

an old, leaky boat
is used to shelter
livestock

a tether keeps the
goat out of the crops

making
soap from ash
and grease

From their raw crops, farmers are
making useful things. They spin and
weave the wool clipped from sheep,
turning it into fine white cloth. Fullers
clean the fabric by treading it underfoot in
baths of urine. Recent settlers are planting
a new crop, wheat. Hand-turned mills crush
the grain to make flour for baking bread.

The simple hut has grown bigger. Its farmer
owner has added an extra room. The yard
outside smells of ripe olives. At its centre,
a patient donkey trudges round in circles
to drive a large olive press. The green
oil that runs from it is an ingredient in
delicious dishes. The pulp left behind
makes animal feed. The dried stones
help to fuel the cooking fire.

Labourers rebuild the
city wall, replacing soft lava
blocks with sturdy limestone.

9

The town develops 300BCE

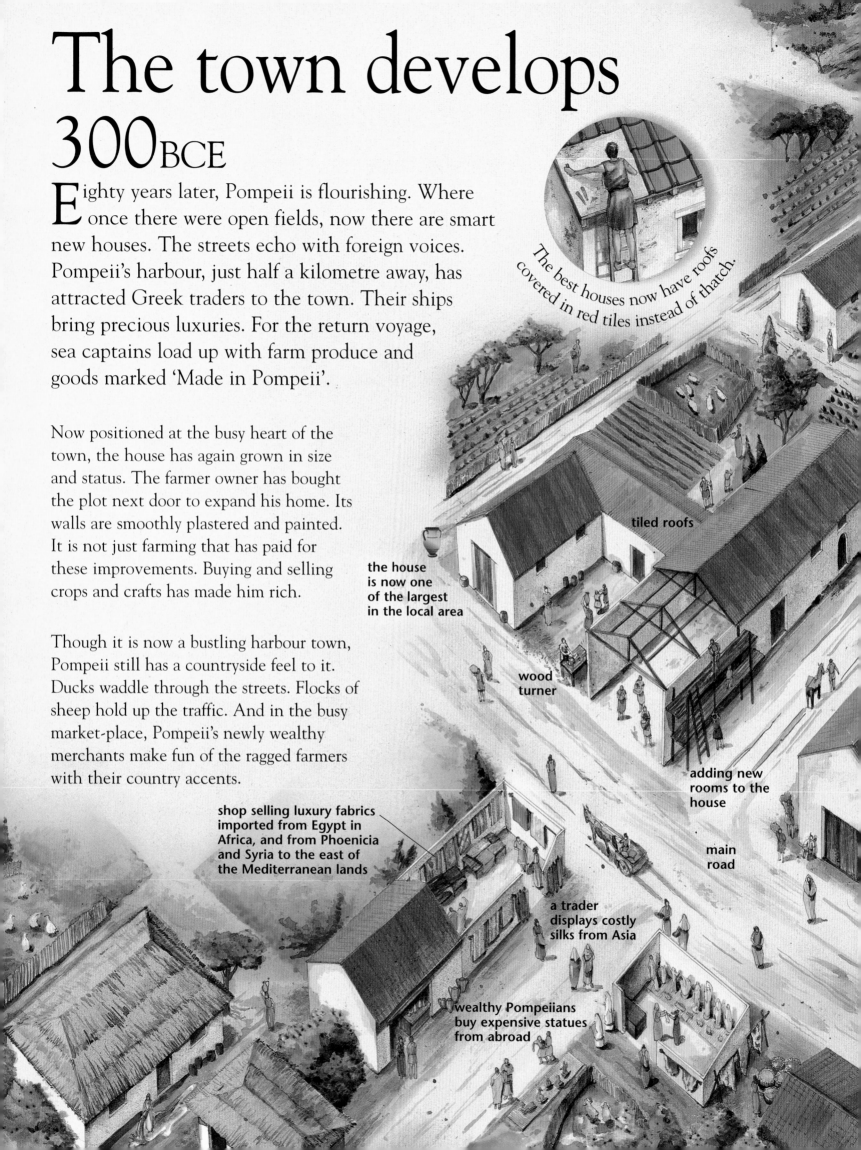

Eighty years later, Pompeii is flourishing. Where once there were open fields, now there are smart new houses. The streets echo with foreign voices. Pompeii's harbour, just half a kilometre away, has attracted Greek traders to the town. Their ships bring precious luxuries. For the return voyage, sea captains load up with farm produce and goods marked 'Made in Pompeii'.

Now positioned at the busy heart of the town, the house has again grown in size and status. The farmer owner has bought the plot next door to expand his home. Its walls are smoothly plastered and painted. It is not just farming that has paid for these improvements. Buying and selling crops and crafts has made him rich.

Though it is now a bustling harbour town, Pompeii still has a countryside feel to it. Ducks waddle through the streets. Flocks of sheep hold up the traffic. And in the busy market-place, Pompeii's newly wealthy merchants make fun of the ragged farmers with their country accents.

The best houses now have roofs covered in red tiles instead of thatch.

tiled roofs

the house is now one of the largest in the local area

wood turner

adding new rooms to the house

main road

shop selling luxury fabrics imported from Egypt in Africa, and from Phoenicia and Syria to the east of the Mediterranean lands

a trader displays costly silks from Asia

wealthy Pompeiians buy expensive statues from abroad

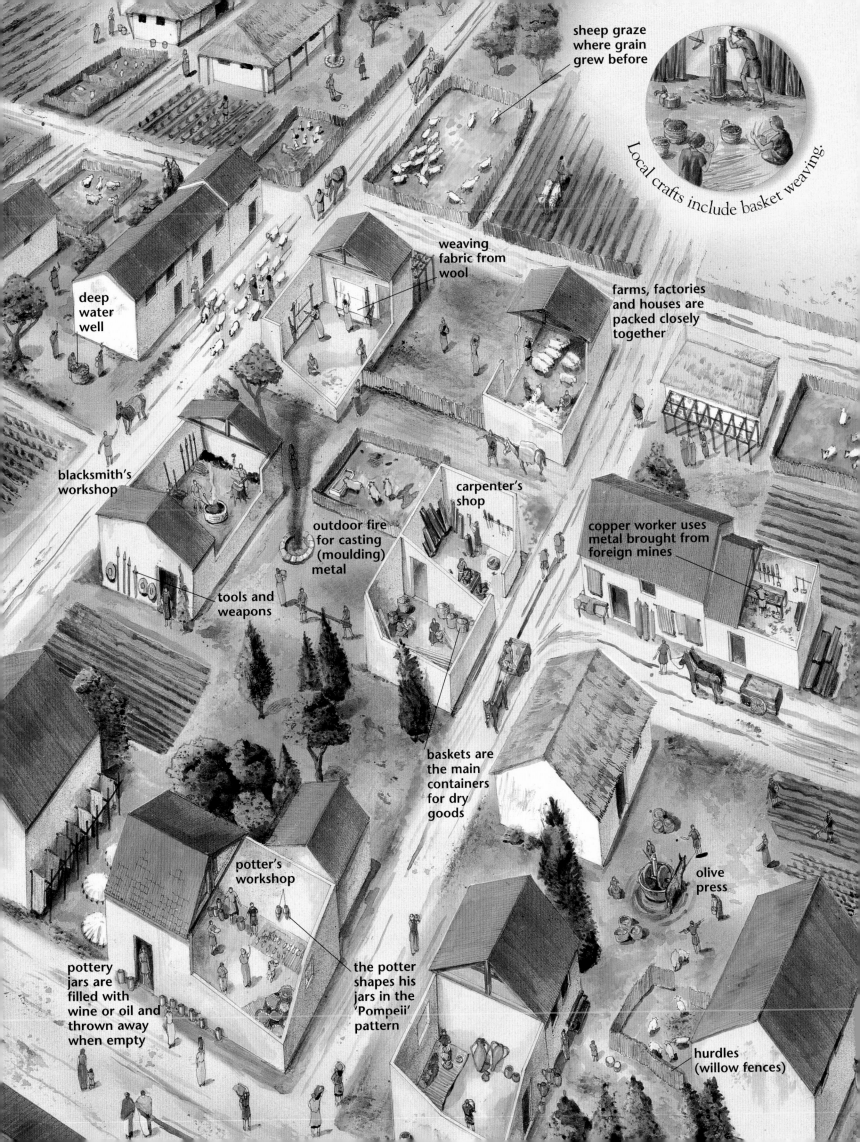

sheep graze where grain grew before

Local crafts include basket weaving.

deep water well

weaving fabric from wool

farms, factories and houses are packed closely together

blacksmith's workshop

carpenter's shop

outdoor fire for casting (moulding) metal

copper worker uses metal brought from foreign mines

tools and weapons

baskets are the main containers for dry goods

potter's workshop

olive press

pottery jars are filled with wine or oil and thrown away when empty

the potter shapes his jars in the 'Pompeii' pattern

hurdles (willow fences)

The house prospers 150BCE

Not everyone in Pompeii lives in a big house. As the city grows, poorer families rent tiny flats in cenacula (apartment blocks). The shops below open onto the street. Cheaply built, the blocks are cracking and crumbling.

The house on the other side of the street is now very fashionable. The wealthy owner has added a small garden. Decorators are painting the columns that hold up the tiled roof surrounding it. Called a peristyle, the garden is a cool, peaceful haven from the bustle of the street outside.

At the front of the house is a seafood bar. A freed slave (freedman) runs it, renting his shop from his former owner. Customers choose their food from the warmed jars set into the marble counter. Visitors to the town are not the only customers. Few of the apartments opposite have kitchens, so their tenants buy takeaways here.

families share tiny rooms in an apartment building

shops

getting rid of dirt and dust

foreign traders from Pompeii's docks

snack bar

In crowded apartments, the kitchen, dining room, bedroom and bathroom are all in the same room.

badly built apartments are in danger of collapsing

stone blocks in the road are shaped to fit tightly together

wealthy houses with lavish peristyle gardens

Hungry street children steal food from the open counters of the snack bar.

peristyle (courtyard garden)

people drive carts on the right-hand side of the road

walls and columns painted to look like expensive marble

slaves tend the shrubs

rubbish and filth will be swept away by the rain

once a farm house, this building is now a fashionable town house

the owner greets visitors in the tablinum (office)

atrium (paved courtyard)

seafood bar

freedman owner of the bar

fresh fish cooked to order

visitors buy snacks and local people buy takeaways to eat at home

13

Inside the atrium
100BCE

Every grand house in Pompeii has an atrium – a paved courtyard. Its roof drains rainwater into a central pool. The pool overflows into a buried cistern (tank), which supplies drinking water. The atrium is not just a way to collect water. It cools the surrounding rooms. The atrium's size and decoration shows off the owner's wealth.

fake windows are painted on the walls

the peristyle can be seen from the atrium

the house owner greets a visitor

a slave attends to the waiting clients

tablinum (office)

pet bird

the atrium is a less private area where official callers can wait to see the house owner

rainwater falls into the impluvium (pool) to keep the atrium cool, then overflows into a cistern below to be collected as drinking water

access hole leading to the cistern

Drawing water from the cistern is easier than using the deep wells in town.

expensive mosaic floor

The shady atrium is the centre of life in the house. Children play on the cool tiles around the shallow pool. Slaves come to fetch water. The master of the house greets visitors in the tablinum, a room that overlooks the atrium. The overhanging roof of the atrium means that this 'outdoor room' is comfortable, even during the rare summer storms.

In a side room a Greek slave teaches the children. They learn reading and writing by chanting poems and copying letters onto wax-coated boards. Naughty children are caned across the hand or whipped over the back. The teacher reminds them of what the Greek thinker Aristotle once said... 'all learning is painful'.

the walls are painted to look like expensive marble

thick double doors close off the school room from the noisy atrium

Poorer children are taught by fellow Pompeii citizens in outdoor 'street schools'.

archways show off the whole house to people looking in from the street

children play with dolls, balls and wooden pull-along animals

a Greek slave serves as a pedagogus (teacher) for wealthy boys at home

the blunt end of the stylus (writing tool) rubs out errors in the wax-covered writing board

15

The city under attack
89 BCE

An urgent message rings through the streets. 'The Romans are at the gates!' As soon as this news reaches the house, giant catapults start to pound the roofs with rocks. The people of Pompeii are fighting rule from Rome, demanding equal treatment with Roman people. The Romans have sent their army to show they still control Italy.

fights break out in every street between Roman soldiers and Pompeii's rebels

the house suffers terrible damage

seafood bar

fires spread from the damaged bakery

thermopolium (hot food bar)

Springs made of animal gristle power the Roman ballista (stone-hurler).

stepping stones

citizens escaping from danger

cart carrying weapons and supplies for the Roman army

Roman soldiers march in

The attack terrifies the family in the house, but it angers them, too. They do not want to be second-class citizens. So, like people in other Italian towns, they are fighting the mighty Roman army. They were waiting for the attack, and have stored weapons to fight back. But they know they have little chance of winning the battle.

the ballista fires grapefruit-sized rocks, which can cause a lot of damage

clay tiles shatter easily

rocks batter down walls and roofs, forcing people to flee from their houses

Pompeii's rebels paint directions on the walls for those defending the city.

The Roman army is well trained, with the very best weapons and equipment. They soon surround Pompeii and demand that the citizens surrender. Their catapults smash buildings. Flaming missiles start fires. As the city walls crumble, so too does the rebellion. Columns of soldiers march through the streets. Pompeii is defeated! Fearing revenge attacks, the family abandons the house.

fleeing citizens

rebels fight back

17

After the war 82 BCE

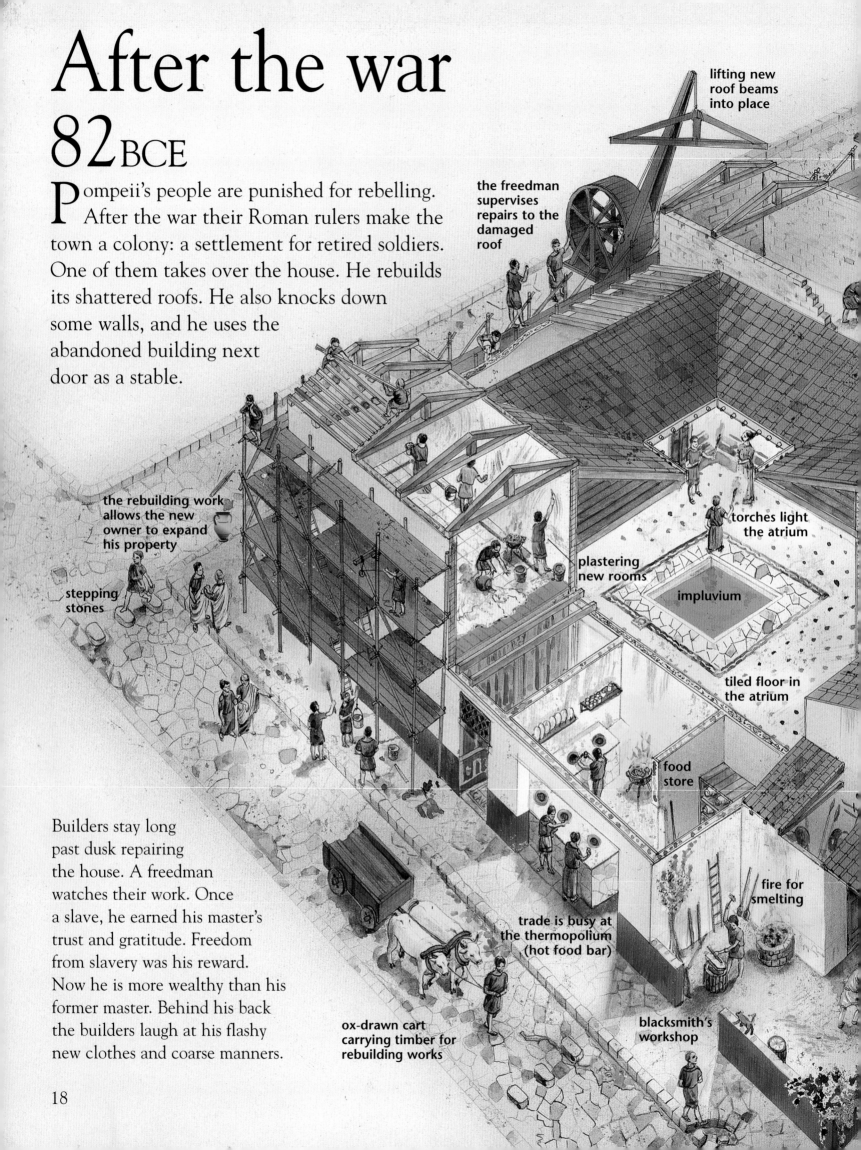

Pompeii's people are punished for rebelling. After the war their Roman rulers make the town a colony: a settlement for retired soldiers. One of them takes over the house. He rebuilds its shattered roofs. He also knocks down some walls, and he uses the abandoned building next door as a stable.

Builders stay long past dusk repairing the house. A freedman watches their work. Once a slave, he earned his master's trust and gratitude. Freedom from slavery was his reward. Now he is more wealthy than his former master. Behind his back the builders laugh at his flashy new clothes and coarse manners.

lifting new roof beams into place

the freedman supervises repairs to the damaged roof

the rebuilding work allows the new owner to expand his property

stepping stones

torches light the atrium

plastering new rooms

impluvium

tiled floor in the atrium

food store

fire for smelting

trade is busy at the thermopolium (hot food bar)

ox-drawn cart carrying timber for rebuilding works

blacksmith's workshop

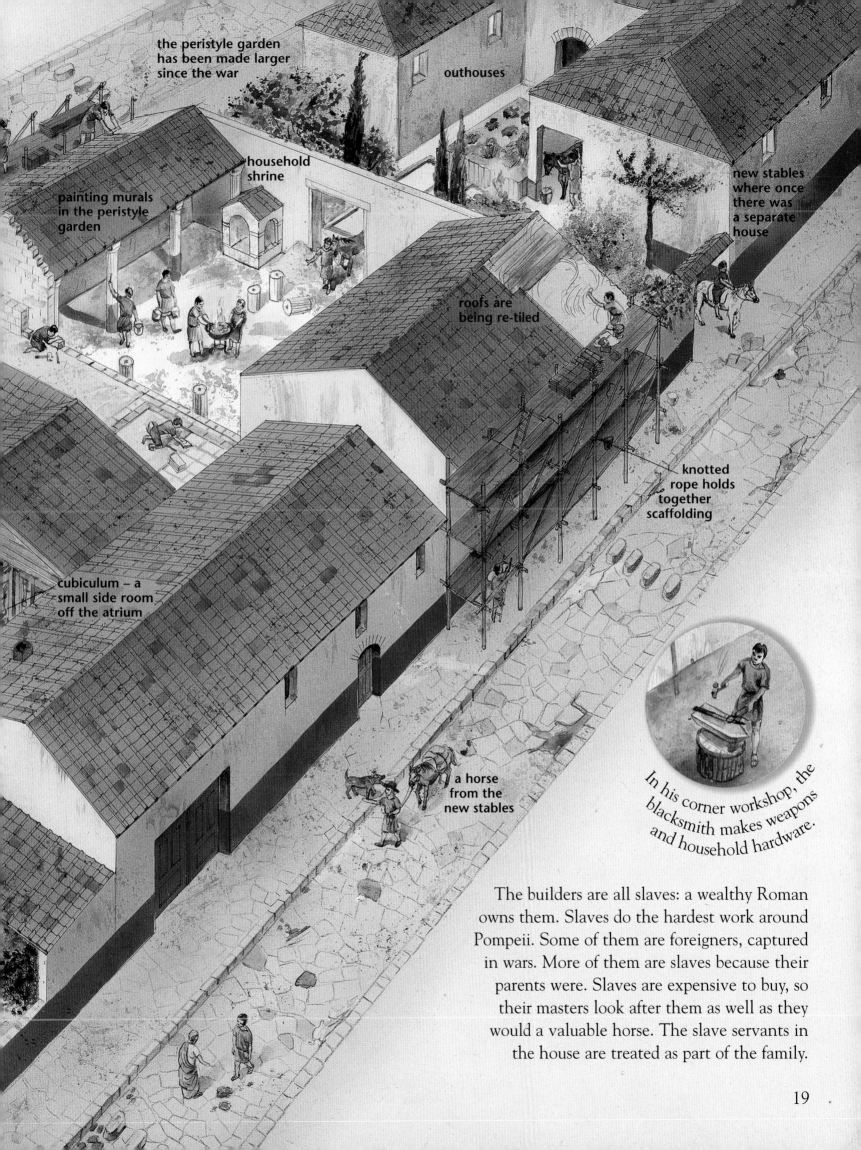

the peristyle garden has been made larger since the war

outhouses

household shrine

new stables where once there was a separate house

painting murals in the peristyle garden

roofs are being re-tiled

knotted rope holds together scaffolding

cubiculum – a small side room off the atrium

a horse from the new stables

In his corner workshop, the blacksmith makes weapons and household hardware.

The builders are all slaves: a wealthy Roman owns them. Slaves do the hardest work around Pompeii. Some of them are foreigners, captured in wars. More of them are slaves because their parents were. Slaves are expensive to buy, so their masters look after them as well as they would a valuable horse. The slave servants in the house are treated as part of the family.

A growing city
10 CE

Ninety-two years on, the quiet street outside the house has grown into a busy highway. The ox-carts, donkeys and people moving along the road are all heading for the forum. At the western end of Pompeii, the forum is in the most important part of the city. Around this grand square stand markets, government offices, temples and baths.

The forum shows just how 'Roman' Pompeii has become. All around you can see the Latin language of the Roman colonists who settled here after the war. It is on food and fabric stalls, on government notices, and even in the graffiti scrawled on lavatory walls. The Romans brought their religion with them, too, adding new temples dedicated to their gods and goddesses.

horse and chariot speeding along a quiet street

Warm-air heating, called a hypocaust, keeps the floor and water warm at the forum baths.

street trader's stall selling foreign goods

grain market

street traders

a one-way traffic system is now operating in the city, to prevent too many accidents

wealthy houses with large, lavish peristyle gardens

bakery

Temple of Apollo

Stretched canvas shades the audience at the outdoor theatre.

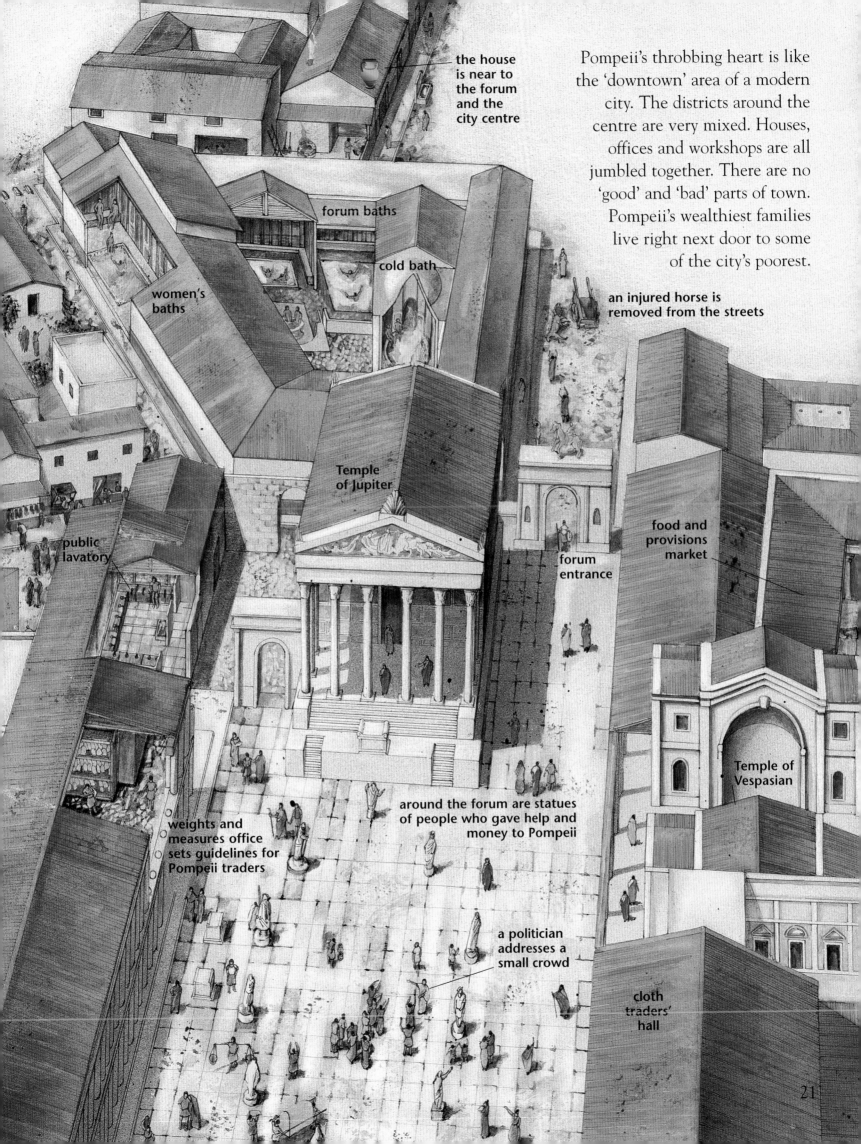

the house is near to the forum and the city centre

Pompeii's throbbing heart is like the 'downtown' area of a modern city. The districts around the centre are very mixed. Houses, offices and workshops are all jumbled together. There are no 'good' and 'bad' parts of town. Pompeii's wealthiest families live right next door to some of the city's poorest.

forum baths

cold bath

women's baths

an injured horse is removed from the streets

Temple of Jupiter

food and provisions market

public lavatory

forum entrance

weights and measures office sets guidelines for Pompeii traders

around the forum are statues of people who gave help and money to Pompeii

Temple of Vespasian

a politician addresses a small crowd

cloth traders' hall

21

The house at its peak

60CE

Glittering with marble mosaics and echoing to the splash of cooling fountains, the house has become luxurious, calm and comfortable. From the street door, visitors look through enchanting open spaces and rooms to distant gardens. The wealthy family living here has made the house magnificent. Within its walls they feel safe from all harm.

Water has helped make the house grander than ever before. Since an aqueduct (water channel) reached Pompeii, rich families have had water piped into their homes. The water spouts from fountains and keeps the gardens green, even in the dry mid-summer.

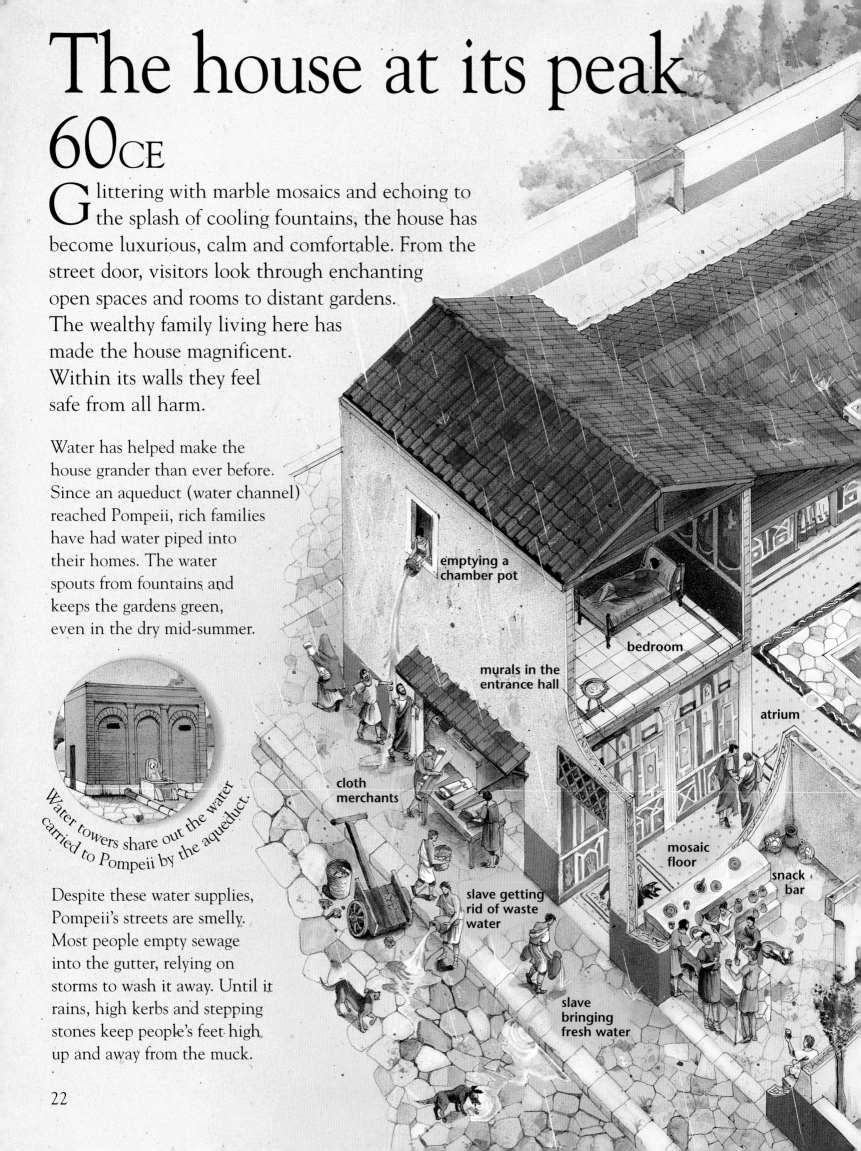

Water towers share out the water carried to Pompeii by the aqueduct.

Despite these water supplies, Pompeii's streets are smelly. Most people empty sewage into the gutter, relying on storms to wash it away. Until it rains, high kerbs and stepping stones keep people's feet high up and away from the muck.

emptying a chamber pot

murals in the entrance hall

bedroom

atrium

cloth merchants

mosaic floor

snack bar

slave getting rid of waste water

slave bringing fresh water

22

slave throwing out excess water from a neighbouring house

a second peristyle garden

curved roof tiles channel rainwater into an opening in the roof called the compluvium

bedroom

main peristyle garden, with fountain

dining room

greeting a visitor in the tablinum

kitchen

slave fetching water from the cistern

lavatory

impluvium collects the rainwater

storage room

street kitchen

eating area

cubiculum

bakery

bread oven

slaves turn mill stones to grind grain

blacksmith's workshop

poorer people collect water from street spouts

stepping stones

23

the peristyle garden is a private space for friends and family

slaves tend the garden and pick flowers for the banquet

slaves bringing more food

jar of garum – a costly cooking sauce made of rotted fish guts

lavatory

plucking poultry

a second kitchen serves the outdoor snack bar

A banquet
60CE

As the sun sets, the sound of music and laughter disturbs the quiet street. There is a banquet in the house in honour of an important politician. Free-flowing wine has made the guests very relaxed. They lounge on the three gently sloping couches of the triclinium (dining room). The meal is almost at an end.

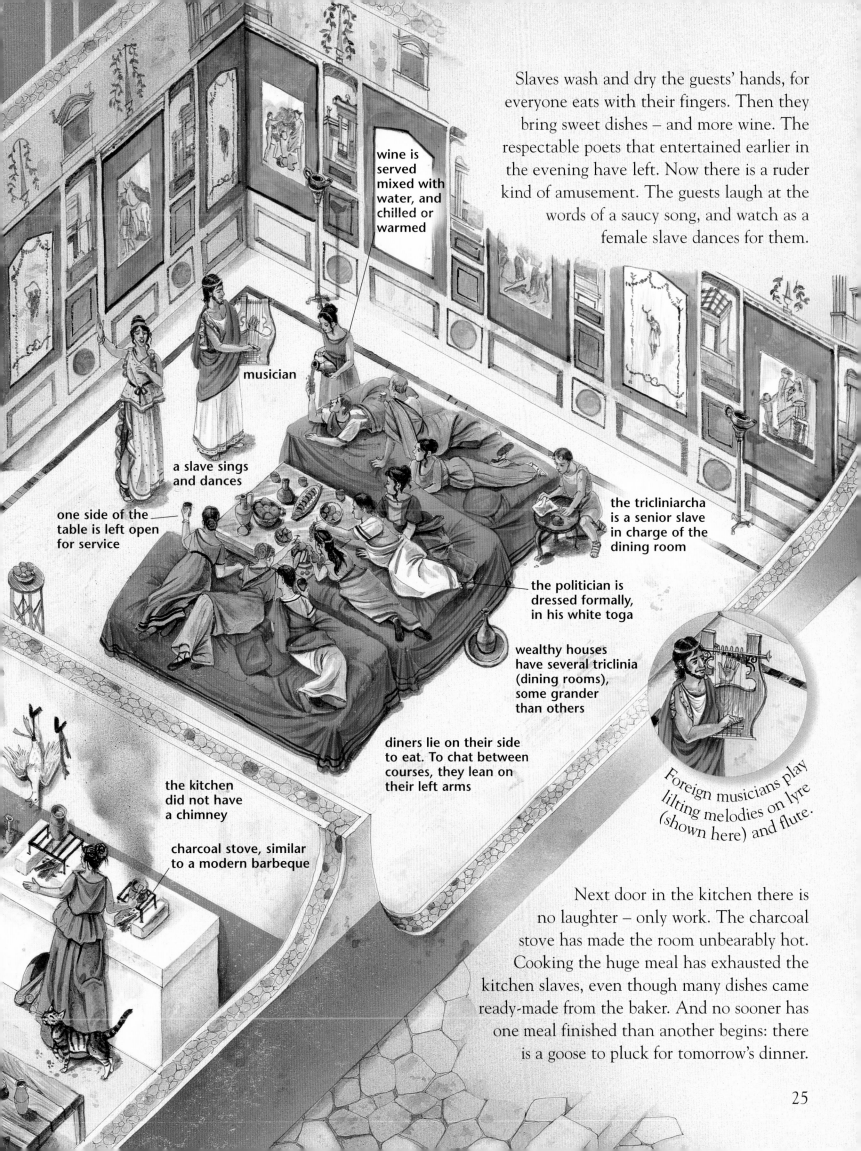

Slaves wash and dry the guests' hands, for everyone eats with their fingers. Then they bring sweet dishes – and more wine. The respectable poets that entertained earlier in the evening have left. Now there is a ruder kind of amusement. The guests laugh at the words of a saucy song, and watch as a female slave dances for them.

wine is served mixed with water, and chilled or warmed

musician

a slave sings and dances

one side of the table is left open for service

the tricliniarcha is a senior slave in charge of the dining room

the politician is dressed formally, in his white toga

wealthy houses have several triclinia (dining rooms), some grander than others

diners lie on their side to eat. To chat between courses, they lean on their left arms

Foreign musicians play lilting melodies on lyre (shown here) and flute.

the kitchen did not have a chimney

charcoal stove, similar to a modern barbeque

Next door in the kitchen there is no laughter – only work. The charcoal stove has made the room unbearably hot. Cooking the huge meal has exhausted the kitchen slaves, even though many dishes came ready-made from the baker. And no sooner has one meal finished than another begins: there is a goose to pluck for tomorrow's dinner.

The earthquake
62 CE

It starts as a tremor, just enough to rattle the plates in the kitchen and send a ripple across the pools. Nobody is worried. The people of Pompeii are used to earthquakes. Sometimes they crack a wall or two. Few do any real harm. Anyway, it is February. There has never been a bad earthquake in the winter. Until now...

When the earthquake strikes it feels as if the fire god Vulcan has picked up the house and shaken it. The atrium columns sway. Mosaic floors buck like angry horses. Everybody falls to the ground. This is just the start. Amid a terrifying roar a great crack opens up in the road outside. A dog tumbles into it.

After the earthquake, people return to their houses to rescue those trapped in the rubble.

Then, as quickly as it appeared, the crack closes up. The walls of the triclinium totter and fall. Others are split with many cracks. Red clay roof tiles slide off and shatter on the ground. Water stops flowing from the fountains. Instead, it gushes out of holes in the road – at least until the aqueduct runs dry.

the badly-built apartments suffer the worst damage

fires start where the earthquake has up-turned cooking stoves

trees fall down

weak walls collapse

a slave salvages his belongings and heads for safety

a foreign trader flees to the harbour

an escaped guard-dog chases the citizens

children are carried away from danger

birds fly from the quivering trees

balconies collapse and fall into the street below

people run from damaged buildings

rooms around the peristyle are destroyed

falling tiles injure people in the streets

rubble buries slaves trapped inside houses

thieves take advantage of the chaos

the walls and roofs of the house suffer the most damage

deep cracks open up in Pompeii's streets

cracks open up, even in the stoutest walls

a frightened horse bolts

water floods out from damaged pipes

people are rescued from collapsing buildings

27

After the earthquake 70CE

Eight years after the earthquake, Pompeii has still not quite returned to normal. There are cracked walls and collapsed buildings on every street. The lives of some of Pompeii's people will never be the same again. Some left the city for good, terrified of another tremor. The poorer people stayed on. Where else could they go? And for some, the earthquake was a golden opportunity.

The earthquake did not destroy every building in the city. But many were so badly damaged that their owners could not afford to repair them. Wealthy next-door neighbours snapped up the abandoned homes. So the house at the crossroads is now even bigger and grander.

Builders have grown wealthy. With everyone desperate for repairs, they are able to double their fees. In cheaper houses they make hurried repairs to cover the worst of the damage. But Pompeii's rich want their homes rebuilt more lavishly than before. There is even a new fashion in decoration. Now artists paint blank walls to look like windows and doors with views out onto fantastic landscapes.

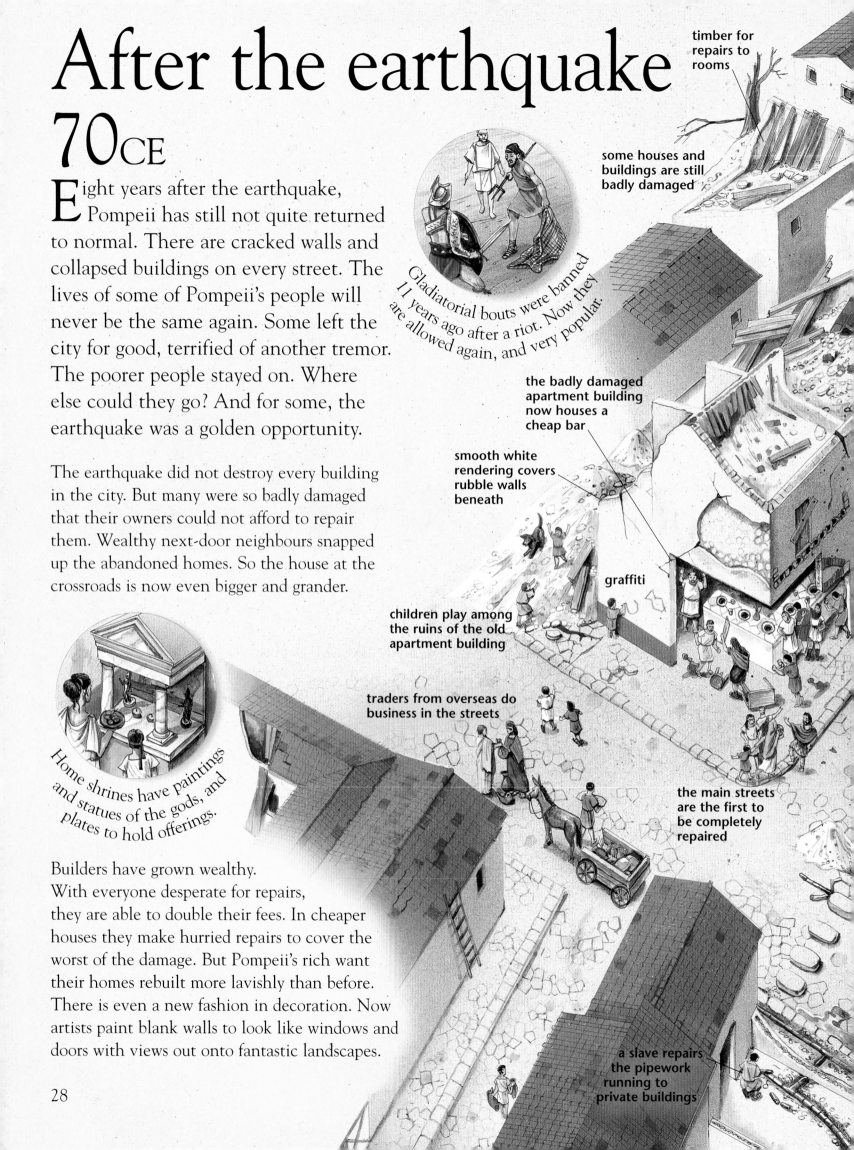

Gladiatorial bouts were banned 11 years ago after a riot. Now they are allowed again, and very popular.

Home shrines have paintings and statues of the gods, and plates to hold offerings.

timber for repairs to rooms

some houses and buildings are still badly damaged

the badly damaged apartment building now houses a cheap bar

smooth white rendering covers rubble walls beneath

graffiti

children play among the ruins of the old apartment building

traders from overseas do business in the streets

the main streets are the first to be completely repaired

a slave repairs the pipework running to private buildings

28

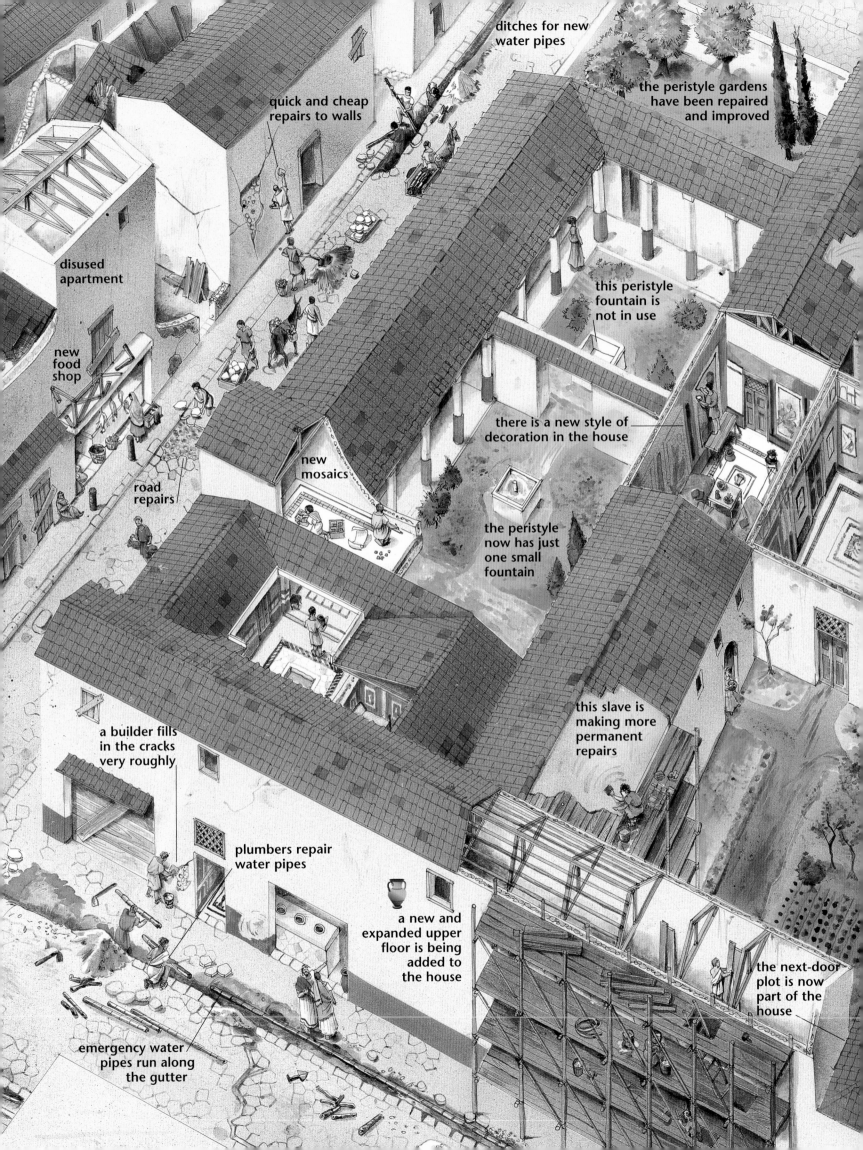

ditches for new water pipes

quick and cheap repairs to walls

the peristyle gardens have been repaired and improved

disused apartment

this peristyle fountain is not in use

new food shop

there is a new style of decoration in the house

road repairs

new mosaics

the peristyle now has just one small fountain

a builder fills in the cracks very roughly

this slave is making more permanent repairs

plumbers repair water pipes

a new and expanded upper floor is being added to the house

emergency water pipes run along the gutter

the next-door plot is now part of the house

the electrically charged cloud causes a lightning storm

the mushroom-shaped cloud is filled with ash, a type of eruption known as 'Plinian' – named after Pliny the Younger, who witnessed the Vesuvius eruption and described it in a letter

fires break out in the woodland around the city

escaping on a horse

piles of ash make doors impossible to open

the mounting ash makes it difficult for people to escape

shopkeepers collect as many valuable items as they can carry

fleeing citizens cover their heads

before the eruption, earthquakes caused walls to crack

ash soon buries those who fall

people choke on the ash and poisonous gases in the air

30

The eruption 79CE

Small, strange things make the morning of the 24th August 79CE different from other mornings. Wells dry up. Dogs howl. All the birds stop singing. There are tremors in the earth. At the time, nobody thinks of these things as warning signs. After all, tremors are not unusual during a Pompeii summer. But then, at the hottest part of the day, it happens. With an awful, deafening roar, Vesuvius explodes.

People use cushions and baskets to protect themselves from falling cinders and lumps of lava.

The eruption blasts the top part of the mountain high into the sky, blotting out the sun. Half an hour later, ash begins to fall on Pompeii like hot, black snow. So much ash! In two hours it is knee-deep. The terrified population flees, grabbing whatever they can carry. By dusk, most people have left Pompeii.

Most... but not all. The rich owner of the house at the crossroads stays indoors, fearing looters will rob him. Other people take cover inside the nearest building, hoping they will be safe. Shopkeepers who return to collect their gold delay their escape for too long. By dawn all are dead, killed by falling roofs, by poisonous gas from the mountain, or fried by the fiery cloud that rolls over the city.

the ash cloud blocks out light from the sun, as if day has suddenly turned to night

the falling ash turns to hot cinders, causing fires to break out

ash and pumice form a thick layer on roofs

a roof collapses under the weight of ash and pumice

the house owner is woken by his loyal slaves, who tell him the city is being evacuated

the owner of the seafood bar takes shelter from the raining ash

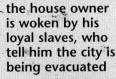

a dog chokes and struggles above the rising ash

A city buried 100CE

W here a bustling, glittering city once stood, now there is only a desert of ash. A river and the sea lapped at Pompeii's walls, but not any more. The eruption changed the coast and diverted the river. The nearby town of Herculaneum is buried even deeper than Pompeii. The disaster alarms all the Roman people. Even the emperor, Titus, comes to inspect the damage.

Titus can do little but watch as Pompeii's people try to salvage what they can from the ruins. They can just see the outline of the buried city's streets. Some make tunnels to recover precious possessions they left behind, or find bronze statues from the forum. Soon, though, the city becomes a quarry, as builders dig up marble and even paving stones.

Some of their discoveries are not so welcome. Soon after the eruption the ash hardened around those who did not escape in time. Now their corpses have rotted to skeletons. The salvage workers find the bones inside body-shaped hollows at the bottom of the ash. They shudder, and offer a quick prayer to Vulcan, the Roman fire god.

The eruption has greatly enlarged the crater of Mount Vesuvius, and the mighty volcano is once more at rest.

digging through to buried buildings in the forum

new vegetation sprouts out of the soil, which is very fertile due to all the ash from the eruption

Larger tunnels are dug through to parts of the forum area, to find valuable public items such as statues.

Valuable items are recovered from the forum and returned to Rome as part of the official salvage operation.

the tunnels are filled in once items have been salvaged

statues and other valuable items are found and removed

the top part of a temple in the forum has been uncovered

the top of a tower sticks up through the ash, and is raided for building materials

The lower part of the house is still buried under several metres of volcanic ash.

the digging has exposed the remains of the upper storey of the house

this doorway shows where the main entrance into the atrium once was

workers dig down to uncover buried buildings

a farmer plants new vines

a worker collects paving stones

only the tops of walls are visible after the digging

these workers are removing stone and materials to be used in new buildings

Pompeii forgotten 1689CE

Sixteen centuries have passed since Vesuvius erupted so violently. The local people now call the neighbourhood 'la Città' (the city). They do not even remember Pompeii's name. The farmers who grow apricots and vines on the rich black soil never suspect that the roots of their crops curl around beautiful statues in the peristylium of the house at the crossroads.

However... from time to time, Pompeii reveals a handful of its secrets, reminding Italians of the lost civilization buried beneath their feet. In around 1600, labourers digging a canal cut through the lower floors of Pompeii's buildings. But nobody pays much attention to the coins they find, or to the letters carved on the stones they dig up.

vineyard

the volcanic soil is rich in minerals and ideal for agriculture

wine press

the farm owner

the farmers keep horses for pulling carts and ploughs

rain soaks quickly into the light soil, so the crops and vines will need extra water from the new well

the soil is light and easy to till by hand

the local residents no longer fear the volcano's power

Half a century ago, in 1631, Vesuvius exploded again, making its crater three times bigger.

plants in the area soon recovered from the light ash shower from the 1631 eruption

apricot and cherry trees

the farm houses are built from Pompeii stone, salvaged centuries ago

sowing seeds for this year's crops

ploughing and hoeing the fields sometimes turns up fragments of masonry

some of the tracks between farms still follow the route of Pompeii's roads

the remains of the house at the crossroads lie buried beneath these fields

Workers digging the well cut through the ash layers left by the eruption of 79CE.

vineyard

the well is very deep because the water is far below ground

a stone lining stops the well from collapsing

In 1689 farm workers digging a well find a stone inscribed 'Decurio Pompeiis'. They think this may refer to a Roman statesman called Pompey. The farm owner shows a historian, from the city of Naples, who knows of Pompeii's destruction from a Roman description of the eruption. They study the well together, and dig up some rusty keys, but the historian is still not sure what they have found. 'This stone is from the ruins of a country house near Pompeii', he tells the farmer.

buckets and carts are used to clear away soil dug from the well

35

before scientific archaeology begins, in the 19th century, all excavations are like those going on here in Pompeii

these scholars are not interested in the pattern of Pompeii's walls – they are simply looking for precious items

wooden panels prevent earth from falling in while a ruin is being explored

groups of prison convicts are forced to help with the digging

Pompeii's famous wall paintings, inside, suddenly make Roman-style decoration very fashionable in Europe

wealthy Europeans visit to watch excavators stage 'discoveries' of precious objects reburied earlier

Treasure hunters 1750CE

In the spring of 1748, Giacopo Martorelli is sure he will discover Pompeii: 'It lies beneath la Città!', he tells anyone who will listen. Martorelli, a professor of Greek literature, is a very persuasive man. Digging begins in April and success comes quickly: the workers discover beautiful wall paintings, a Roman helmet, oil lamps and coins.

An inscription on a stone, found in 1763, proves beyond doubt that la Civita lies on the site of Pompeii.

Within three weeks they find the first skeleton, and a handful of gold and silver. This small heap of money encourages a hunt for more, and frantic digging begins. The search for Pompeii turns into a treasure hunt.

In the years that follow, some amazing finds are made. Shovels strike sparks from the stones as workers uncover the house at the crossroads. But for the scholars in charge, valuable ornaments are what matter. Whenever they stop finding beautiful paintings and gold or silver statues, they simply fill in their holes and move on.

Carelessness, rivalry and greed scatter Pompeii's riches. The king of Naples takes the best of the art for his private collections. The less impressive pieces are deliberately smashed so that they cannot be sold illegally. Criminals shovelling ash, as part of their punishment, pocket small treasures. And nobody bothers to keep a record of what they find, or where it lies.

two workers fill in a ruin after removing its treasures

ash has preserved the seafood bar attached to the house

the position of these ruins is not recorded – later on in the 18th century, more detailed plans of the finds are made

Scholars are allowed to study the finds, but only if they have been specially invited by the king.

wheelbarrows are used to move the ash away and dump it nearby

37

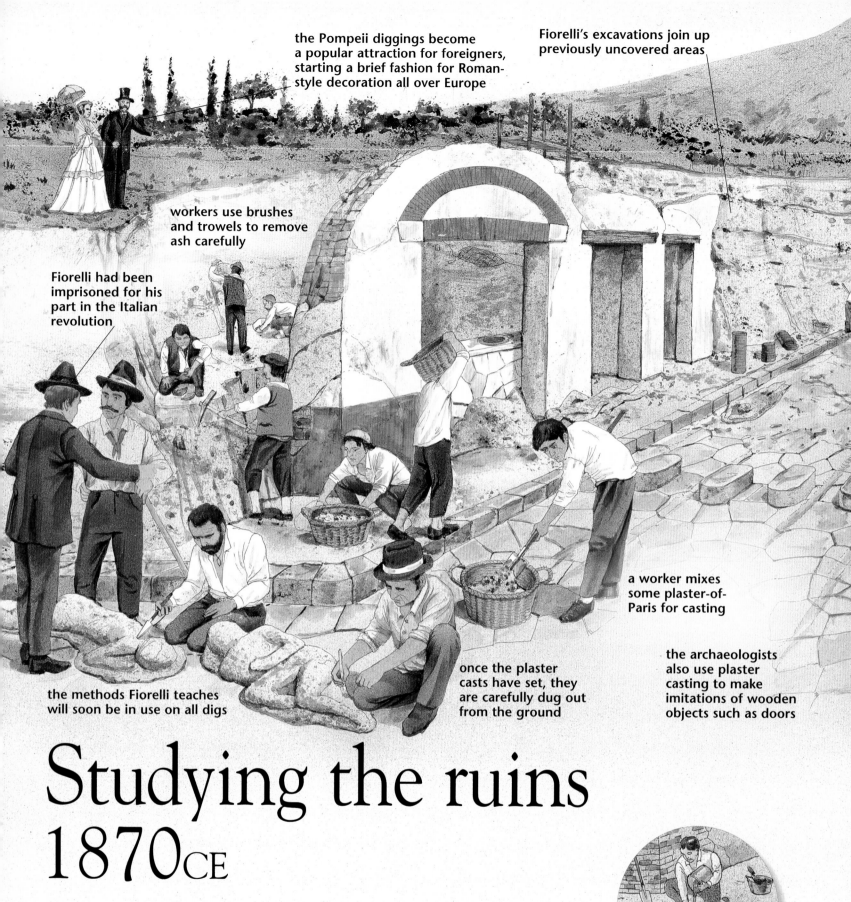

the Pompeii diggings become a popular attraction for foreigners, starting a brief fashion for Roman-style decoration all over Europe

Fiorelli's excavations join up previously uncovered areas

workers use brushes and trowels to remove ash carefully

Fiorelli had been imprisoned for his part in the Italian revolution

a worker mixes some plaster-of-Paris for casting

the methods Fiorelli teaches will soon be in use on all digs

once the plaster casts have set, they are carefully dug out from the ground

the archaeologists also use plaster casting to make imitations of wooden objects such as doors

Studying the ruins 1870CE

Removing Pompeii's artefacts, without describing where they were found, is disastrous. It robs Italians of their history. The excavations are better recorded in the 19th century, but scientific study begins only in 1861, after a revolution unites Italy's many kingdoms as a single country. The king of this new nation is Vittorio Emanuele (1820–78).

The archaeologists use liquid plaster-of-Paris to make casts of the corpses. It sets hard in minutes.

Fiorelli gives each region, street block and door an 'address' to help with the recording of finds in these areas

skeletons are found in and around the house and the seafood bar

this cast is of a dog that died outside the seafood bar

the body casts show where people fell as they tried to escape or protect themselves

VI. viii. 4

earth and ash are taken off the site in wheelbarrows and carts

the archaeologists work on one street block at a time

the plaster peels off where the flesh is thin, revealing skulls and knee-caps

an archaeologist makes a written note of where this body was found, and in what position

The king of Italy puts archaeologist Giuseppe Fiorelli (1823–96) in charge of Pompeii. Fiorelli has exciting new ideas. Under his guidance, experts remove the ash from every room in the house at the crossroads, instead of digging small holes. They make a note of everything they find, however worthless it seems at the time. Fiorelli is a pioneer of stratigraphy – the simple but brilliant idea that the oldest objects are buried deepest in the ground.

The casts of Pompeii's dead, displayed in Fiorelli's museum, fill visitors with sorrow and pity.

Fiorelli also believes that his job is not to find treasure, but to build up a picture of the lives of the people of Pompeii. But it is not life, but death, that makes Fiorelli famous. He notices that Pompeii's skeletons lie inside hollows in the ash. He realizes that the hollows trace the shapes of their rotted bodies. Fiorelli fills the hollows with plaster. Removing the surrounding ash creates realistic casts of Pompeiians at the moment Vesuvius smothered them.

Romantic ruin Today

The grand house in Pompeii echoes with voices once more. Each day, some 7,000 people visit the city. They gaze in wonder at the cobbled roads, preserved houses and colourful mosaic decorations. They stare in silence at the casts of the city's dead. And tour guides retell Pompeii's tragic story – which has not yet ended.

Pompeii is dying once again. The city is huge, and Italy's archaeologists do not have the money to protect it all. In the house at the crossroads, weather destroys the murals. Walls collapse where weeds and trees dislodge masonry. Vandals carve their names in the stone and steal souvenirs.

But the news is not all bad. Tourists buy tickets to visit the Pompeii ruins, and in 1997 a law was passed to ensure that money from ticket sales is spent on improving and caring for the site. New conservation projects are being developed, to preserve the ruins while also exploring areas as yet uncovered. So one day we may have an even better picture of the city where life suddenly stopped almost 2,000 years ago.

the apartment building is easy to recognize by the many doorways leading up from street level

cheap food bar

children play on the stepping stones

the cobbled streets punish those foolish enough to wear high-heeled shoes

Digging up a single fish scale can help archaeologists to work out what Pompeii people ate.

stray dogs roam Pompeii's streets – just as they did before the eruption

archaeologists find big mutton bones in this cheap bar, and the small bones of lamb in the expensive house opposite

40

wooden scaffolds reinforce weak walls and keep visitors at a safe distance

peristyle garden

peristyle garden

marble-effect paint has peeled, showing the cheap brick it covered

tablinum

the peristyle gardens have been planted with flowers and trees again

atrium

parts of the house and the seafood bar have been partially restored to show how they once looked

ruts worn by cart-wheels show which way the traffic flowed

tourists visiting the house at the crossroads learn about its history from a tour guide

The perfectly preserved forum baths are the first stop for many of Pompeii's tourists.

41

Glossary

Words in *italics* refer to other glossary entries.

aqueduct
A trough, bridge or pipe carrying drinking water from a water source to towns and cities.

archaeologist
A scientist who studies *archaeology*.

archaeology
Learning about how people lived in the past by studying what remains of them and the things they built and made.

artefacts
Hand-made objects, often found at archaeological *excavations*.

atrium
A courtyard in a house with a surrounding roof that drains rainwater into a central pool or *impluvium*.

ballista
A giant *catapult* that hurls rocks to batter down walls in warfare.

baths
A public place for washing and relaxation, like today's spas.

blacksmith
Someone who heats and hammers iron to shape it into useful things.

casting
Pouring a liquid into a hollow, so that when the liquid sets solid it copies the shape of the hollow.

catapult
A weapon that uses spring power to hurl rocks or stones at an enemy.

cenacula
Blocks of flats or apartment buildings.

chariot
A fast, two-wheeled horse-drawn war cart for carrying soldiers.

cistern
A large tank for storing drinking water.

(la) Città
'The City' – the name used for the region where Pompeii once stood until the city was uncovered.

Mount Vesuvius lies on the coast of the Bay of Naples, about 9km east of the city of Naples in southern Italy. The volcano last erupted in 1944.

We do not know for sure how the first Pompeii residents lived, but elsewhere in Italy they built round, thatched huts like this one.

colonists
People who set up a place to live in a new land. Sometimes, as with Pompeii, old soldiers were given houses or land as a reward for their services.

compluvium
An open space in the middle of the *atrium*.

cubiculum
An upper-floor bedroom, or a small room off the *atrium* used for meetings or as a library.

Emanuele, Vittorio
Italy's first king of modern times. Born in 1820, he ruled from 1861 until his death 17 years later.

emmer
A kind of edible grass grown to make flour, until wheat replaced it as a food plant.

excavation
An area dug up quickly by treasure hunters, or carefully by *archaeologists*, who record and preserve everything they find.

Fiorelli, Giuseppe
An Italian archaeologist (lived 1823–96) who introduced scientific methods of excavation at Pompeii from 1861.

forum
The market-place and central open space of a Roman town.

freedman
A former *slave* who has been given freedom by his owner.

fresco
A wall-painting made by brushing colours onto wet plaster.

fuller
A worker who treats cloth after weaving to clean and thicken it.

fullery
The place where fullers work.

graffiti
Messages scribbled on walls.

gutter
A trough at the side of a road for collecting rainwater and sometimes sewage.

hurdle
A small fence made from thin, bendy sticks woven together.

hypocaust
A furnace-powered heating system that circulates warm air through channels in walls and under floors, for private houses or public *baths*.

impluvium
The pool in the middle of an *atrium* for collecting and saving rainwater, and for keeping the *atrium* cool.

Roman hosts thought that nine diners was the perfect number to have around a table.

kerb
A row of straight stones at the edge of a road, raised to keep vehicles off the pavement.

lararium
The household *shrine* where the family pray to guardian gods and give small offerings.

Latin
The language of the Roman people, and the basis for many modern European languages.

lava
The molten rock thrown out by a *volcano*.

livestock
Animals kept by farmers for their meat, milk, wool, or work.

lyre
A small harp played by strumming, like playing a guitar.

marble
A type of very hard, beautiful building stone that can be polished until shiny. It was also used in sculpture.

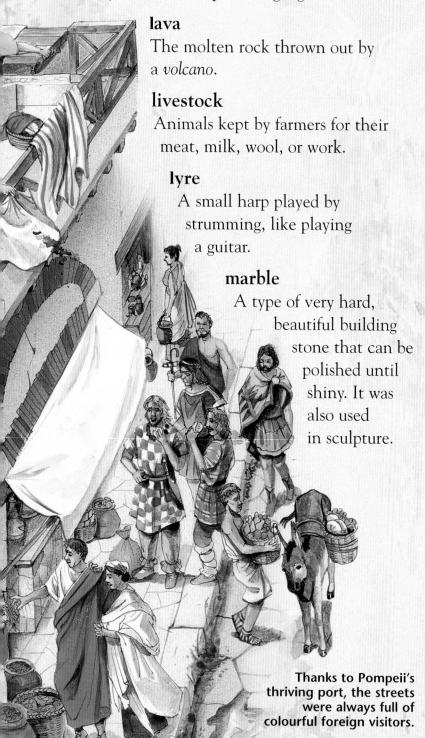

Thanks to Pompeii's thriving port, the streets were always full of colourful foreign visitors.

Martorelli, Giacopo
Professor of Greek writing at Naples university, who in the mid-18th century was among those scholars searching for Pompeii.

masonry
The shaped stones used in building.

mosaic
A picture or pattern made up of many pieces of colourful glass, pottery or stone.

mural
A decorative wall-painting.

Naples
A large port on Italy's west coast, overlooking the bay named after it.

pedagogus
A slave who teaches, looks after and waits upon Roman children.

peristyle garden
A *peristylium* with a garden in the middle.

peristylium
A rectangular courtyard with a porch on one or more sides, supported by columns.

plaster-of-Paris
A white powder that quickly sets hard when mixed with water.

plaster cast
The reversed copy of an object made by *casting* with *plaster-of-Paris*.

Plinian eruption
A *volcanic eruption* that throws ash and dust high into the air, named after the Roman writer who wrote about the eruption of *Vesuvius* in 79CE.

politician
Someone who works in government and law-making, often chosen by the people they serve.

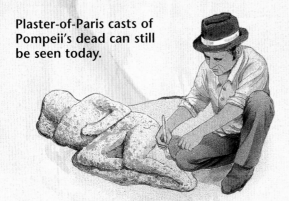

Plaster-of-Paris casts of Pompeii's dead can still be seen today.

pumice
The foamy rock formed when *lava* sets, often light enough to float in water.

restoration
The repair and improvement of something that has been damaged.

scaffolding
A temporary framework set up next to a wall so that workers standing on it can build or repair.

sewage
The liquid and solid waste from lavatories or from washing.

shrine
A small place for prayer and worship in a *temple*, home or street.

slave
Someone owned by, and working for, another person, who is not free to change their life.

smelting
Heating rock to get out the metal it contains.

stratigraphy
The science of judging a buried object's age by comparing it with other objects at the same depth in the ground.

stylus
A pen-like object used to scratch messages.

tablinum
The greeting room in a Roman house between the *atrium* and the *peristylium*.

temple
A place of worship.

tenant
Someone who rents a house or rooms from the owner of a residence.

thatch
A roofing material made of cut plants such as straw or rushes.

thatched roof
A roof covered in *thatch*.

thermopolium
A bar where food and hot or cold drinks are served.

tourist
Someone who tours a country looking at places of interest – or just someone on holiday.

tricliniarcha
A slave in charge of the *triclinium*.

triclinium
A dining room with three sloping couches, each big enough for three people, around a table.

Vesuvius
The *volcano* close to Pompeii that erupted in 79CE, covering the city in ash.

vineyard
A field where grapevines grow.

volcanic eruption
A violent, often destructive outflow of *lava*, ash, gas or other material from a *volcano*.

volcano
A mountain or other place where the earth's liquid core leaks out through gaps in the solid crust.

Vulcan
The Roman fire god.

The sons of wealthy Pompeii citizens were schooled at home.

45

Index

A tour guide retells the dramatic history of Pompeii.

A

amphitheatres 3
aqueducts 22, 42
archaeologists 38, 39, 40, 42
archways 15
armies, Roman 3, 16, 17
artists 28
ash 2, 3, 9, 30, 31, 39
atrium 14, 15, 42

B

ballista 16, 17, 42
baskets 11
baths 20, 21, 41, 42
blacksmiths 18, 19, 42
builders 18, 28, 29

CD

canals 3, 34
carts 13, 16, 18
catapults 16, 17, 42
cement 8
cenacula 12, 42
chariots 20, 42
children 13, 15
cisterns 14, 42
(la) Città 3, 34, 36, 37, 42
cloth *see* fabrics
colonies 18
columns 12, 13

crops 6, 8, 9, 34
cubiculum 19, 43

E

earthquakes 3, 26, 30
Emanuele, Vittorio 38, 43
emmer 6, 43
eruptions 30, 31, 44, 45
excavations 3, 36, 38, 43
excavators 3, 36

F

fabrics 8, 9, 10
farmers 7, 9, 34
farms 6, 9
Fiorelli, Giuseppe 3, 38, 39, 43
fire 16, 17, 26
flour 6, 9
forest 3, 7
forum 20, 32, 41, 43
fountains 22
freedmen 12, 13, 18, 43
fullers 9, 43
fullery 8, 43

G

gardens 12, 13 *see also* peristyle gardens

gladiatorial contests 3, 28
gods 7, 26, 28
graffiti 20, 28, 43
grapes 6
Greeks 2, 3, 10

H

harbour 6, 10
harvest 6
heating 20
Herculaneum 32
hypocausts 20, 43

I

impluvium 14, 23, 43

J

jars 11, 12

K

kitchens 12, 25

L

Latin language 20, 44
limestone 9
lyres 25, 44

M

marble 13, 42
market-places 10
markets 20

Martorelli, Giacopo 36, 44
merchants 10, 43
metal 6, 11
mills 9
mosaics 14, 22, 29, 44
musicians 25

NO

offices 20, 21
olive presses 8, 9
olives 8

P

peristyle gardens 12, 13, 24, 41, 44
pigs 6, 7
pipes 29
plaster casting 38
Pliny the Younger 30
politicians 25, 44
ports 3, 44

Q

quarries 32

R

rebellion 3
rebels 16, 17
religion 20
roads 7, 8, 12
Romans 2, 3, 16
roofs 6, 8, 10, 15, 23

In the years following the eruption of 79CE, Romans visited to salvage precious items and building materials.

S
schools 15
settlers 2, 9
sewage 22, 45
sheep 7, 9, 10, 11
shops 10, 12
shrines 19, 28, 45
skeletons 32, 37, 39
slaves 2, 8, 12, 13, 15, 19, 22, 23, 24, 25, 45
soap, making 9
soil 32, 34
soldiers 2, 3, 16, 17, 18
statues 10, 21, 32
stepping stones 22, 23
stratigraphy 39, 45

T
tablinum 13, 14, 15, 45
takeaways 12
teachers 15
temples 7, 20, 21, 45
thatch 6, 7, 43, 45
theatres 20
tiles 10, 23
timeline (of events in Pompeii's history) 3
Titus, emperor 3, 32
tools 6
tourists 40, 41, 45
traders 10, 12, 28
traffic 20
tricliniarcha 25, 45
triclinium 25, 45
tunnels 32

U
urine baths 8, 9

V
Vesuvius, Mount 2, 3, 6, 7, 30, 31, 32, 42, 45
vines 6, 7, 33, 34
volcanoes 2, 3, 7, 42, 45
Vulcan 32, 45

WXYZ
wall paintings 36, 43, 44
walls of the city 3, 6, 9, 17
water 14, 22, 23
water towers 22
weapons 16, 17, 19, 42
weaving 9, 11
wells 3, 35
wheat 8, 9
wine 6, 11, 25
wolves 6, 7
wood 6
wool 9

Before the eruption that ended life in Pompeii, the city was rocked by an earthquake in 62CE.

Look out for
Through Time:
BEIJING
by Richard Platt
in 2008

In the 4th century BCE Pompeii was already a thriving centre for trade and agriculture.

KINGFISHER

Kingfisher Publications Plc
New Penderel House
283–288 High Holborn
London WC1V 7HZ
www.kingfisherpub.com

Senior editor: Simon Holland
Senior designer: Heidi Appleton
Cover designer: Jo Connor
Consultant: Dr Thorsten Opper, Department of Greek
and Roman Antiquities, The British Museum
Senior production controller: Lindsey Scott
DTP manager: Nicky Studdart
Indexer: Carron Brown

First published by Kingfisher Publications Plc 2007
2 4 6 8 10 9 7 5 3 1

1TR/0507/SHENS/CLSN(CLSN)/158MA/C

ISBN: 978 0 7534 1386 9

Copyright © Kingfisher Publications Plc 2007

A CIP record for this book is available from the British Library.

Printed in Taiwan